HEINEMANN
STATE STUDIES

# Uniquely
# North
# Carolina

Adam McClellan and Martin Wilson

**Heinemann Library**
Chicago, Illinois

© 2004 Heinemann Library
a division of Reed Elsevier Inc.
Chicago, Illinois

Customer Service 888-454-2279

Visit our website at www.heinemannlibrary.com

Designed by Heinemann Library
Printed in China by WKT Company Limited.

08 07 06 05 04
10 9 8 7 6 5 4 3 2 1

**Library of Congress
Cataloging-in-Publication Data**

McClellan, Adam, 1971–
    Uniquely North Carolina / Adam McClellan.
        v. cm.—(Heinemann state studies)
Includes bibliographical references and index.
Contents: Uniquely North Carolina—Climate and
weather—Famous firsts—North Carolina state
symbols—North Carolina's history & people—
Biltmore Estate—North Carolina's state
government—North Carolina's culture—North
Carolina's food—North Carolina folklore and
legends—Sports—North Carolina businesses and
products—Attractions and landmarks.
    ISBN 1-4034-4653-9 (lib. bdg.)—
    ISBN 1-4034-4722-5 (pbk.)
    1. North Carolina—Juvenile literature.
    [1. North Carolina.]
    I. Title. II. Series.
    F254.3.M38 2004
    975.6'04—dc22

2003025448

**Acknowledgments**
Development and photo research by
BOOK BUILDERS LLC

The author and publishers are grateful to the
following for permission to reproduce copyright
material:

Cover photographs by (top, L-R): Bettmann/
Corbis, North Carolina Office of Archives and
History, Joe Sohm/Alamy Images, Courtesy of
North Carolina Division of Tourism, Film, and
Sports Development, Kevin Fleming/Corbis

Special thanks to Jim Sumner of the North Carolina Museum of History for his expert comments
in the preparation of this book.

Every effort has been made to contact copyright
holders of any material reproduced in this book.
Any omissions will be rectified in subsequent
printings if notice is given to the publisher.

Title page (L-R): Alamy, Andre Jenny/Alamy,
North Carolina Office of Archives and History;
pp. 4, 15M, 15B, 16T, 17, 41, 44 Alamy; pp. 5, 7,
14, 21B, 23, 24 Andre Jenny/Alamy Images; p. 6
North Carolina Division of Parks and Recreation;
p. 10 Bettmann/Corbis; pp. 11, 18, 20T, 20B, 21T,
28, 29, 30, 35, 37 North Carolina Office of
Archives and History; p. 12T Joe Sohm/Alamy
Images; p. 13 Winston Fraser/Alamy; p. 15T Courtesy of treehound.com; p; 22T Courtesy of the
Office of United States Senator Elizabeth Dole;
p. 22B Jonathan Kim/Alamy Images; p. 25 Courtesy of North Carolina Division of Tourism, Film,
and Sports Development; p. 31 Sean Rivinus;
p. 32 R. Capozzelli/Heinemann Library; p. 34
Gregg Forwerck/Gale Force Media; p. 36 Dallas
Vogler; p. 38 Martin Heitner/Alamy; p. 40 Kevin
Fleming/Corbis

**Cover Pictures**

**Top** (left to right) North Carolina state flag,
University of North Carolina basketball,
capitol in Raleigh, Wright Brothers in flight
**Main** Cape Hatteras Light Station

Some words are shown in bold, **like this.**
You can find out what they mean by looking
in the glossary.

# Contents

# Uniquely North Carolina

**S**omething that is *unique* is one of a kind. Certainly it can be said that North Carolina is a unique place. It was the site of the first English colony in North America, on Roanoke Island in 1585. North Carolina is also where the world's first airplane took flight, at Kitty Hawk in 1902. The state also has the highest mountain in the eastern United States, Mount Mitchell. Read on to find out more about what makes North Carolina unique.

## ORIGIN OF THE STATE'S NAME

North Carolina was once an English **colony,** from the late 1500s to the late 1700s. The state got its name in 1629, when King Charles I of England granted the land to one of his advisers. The land was known then as *Carolana,* which is Latin for "Land of Charles." The spelling later changed to *Carolina.* In 1712, the colony was split into two parts: north and south.

## MAJOR CITIES

With a population of more than 600,000, Charlotte sits near the South Carolina border in the foothills of the Appalachian Mountains. The city is the second largest banking center in the country, second only to New York City. It is also home to the tallest building in the

*Charlotte is a two-hour drive east of the Blue Ridge Mountains and just over three hours west of the Atlantic Ocean.*

Carolinas, the Bank of America Corporate Center, which has 60 stories and is 871 feet tall. The city is sometimes called the Queen City. This is because, when it was founded in 1768, the people who lived there named it for Queen Charlotte, the wife of King George III.

Raleigh is the capital of North Carolina and its second-largest city, with a population of about 260,000. It was founded in 1792, after the state **legislature** voted to build a new capital city in the center of the state. Raleigh, along with Durham and Chapel Hill, is part of Research Triangle Park. The 7,000-acre park is the largest research park in the United States. Here, scientists and engineers perform cutting-edge research for the government and other important industries.

Wilmington, founded in 1739, sits near the mouth of the Cape Fear River, 28 miles from the Atlantic Ocean. Wilmington played an important role in the **Civil War** (1861–1865), when it was one of only a few **Confederate** ports that were not quickly shut down by the U.S. Navy. Starting in the 1980s, major film companies began establishing studios in Wilmington. EUE/Screen Gems Studios has been in Wilmington for more than seventeen years. It is the largest full-service motion picture facility in the United States east of California. More than 300 films, tele-

*More than 70,000 people live in Wilmington, the largest city in eastern North Carolina.*

vision shows, and commercials have been shot at the studio, including *Dawson's Creek* and *Muppets from Space*.

# North Carolina's Geography and Climate

**N**orth Carolina is bordered by Virginia on the north, Tennessee on the west, Georgia and South Carolina on the south, and the Atlantic Ocean on the east. The state is broken down into three major regions: the Mountain Region, the Piedmont, and the Atlantic Coastal Plain. Each region has distinct climates that reflect the state's varied **topography.**

## THE LAND

The Appalachian Mountain system, which include both the Blue Ridge and Smoky Mountain ranges, runs through the western part of the state. Some of the state's tallest mountains can be found in the Smoky Mountains along the border with Tennessee and the Blue Ridge Mountains in the northwestern part of the

*Mount Mitchell is part of the Black Mountain range. The peak is named for Dr. Elisha Mitchell, who calculated the height of the peak in the mid-1800s.*

state. More than 200 mountains rise above 5,000 feet in the state. Mount Mitchell is the state's highest mountain at 6,684 feet above sea level. It is also the tallest peak east of the Mississippi River.

The Piedmont region makes up the central part of the state. The word *piedmont* is French and means "foot of the mountain." This area takes up about 45 percent of the state's land. The land is covered mostly with low, rolling hills. Much of the Piedmont soil is red clay. The main industries include furniture and **textile** manufacturing. The five largest cities in the state—including Charlotte, Raleigh, and Greensboro—are located in this region. More people live in this region than in the other two combined. In the southeastern corner of the Piedmont are the Sandhills, an area known for its peaches and horse breeding.

In the eastern part of the state lies the Atlantic Coastal Plain, a low, flat area with sandy soil. The land elevation ranges from sea level on the coast to 600 feet high farther west. The Atlantic Coastal Plain is home to many of the state's farms. These farms yield tobacco, peanuts, soybeans, and more.

*The Outer Banks stretch 90 miles along the coast.*

North Carolina has about 300 miles of coastline. Much of this land is protected by a chain of **barrier islands**

known as the Outer Banks. The first English settlement in North America was established on Roanoke Island in the Outer Banks in 1585. These islands can be reached by plane, by boat, or by driving over the many bridges that link the islands to the mainland. Some of the islands are twenty miles wide, while others extend for only a half mile. **Capes,** such as Cape Hatteras, also make up the Outer Banks. These capes have shifting underwater sandbars, or shoals, and used to be very dangerous for passing ships until modern technology made avoiding these shoals easier.

## CLIMATE

North Carolina has a **temperate** climate, though the temperatures often vary by region. The average temperature in the summer ranges from 68°F to 80°F, with the hottest temperatures occurring in the Atlantic Coastal Plain. Summers are hot and sticky throughout much of the state because the air is generally **humid.**

The mountains in the western part of North Carolina affect the state's climate. Due to their elevation, the mountain areas are usually much cooler than the rest of the state in the summer and especially in the winter. In addition, the mountains help keep the rest of the state warmer in the winter by blocking some of the cold air that comes down from the central United States. The winters in the Piedmont and Atlantic Coastal Plain are generally short and mild. The temperatures in the winter range from 36°F to 48°F but are often much colder in the Mountain Region.

## PRECIPITATION—RAIN AND SNOW

North Carolina is a well-watered state. The driest parts of the state are in the Piedmont region. This area gets

# Average Annual Precipitation North Carolina

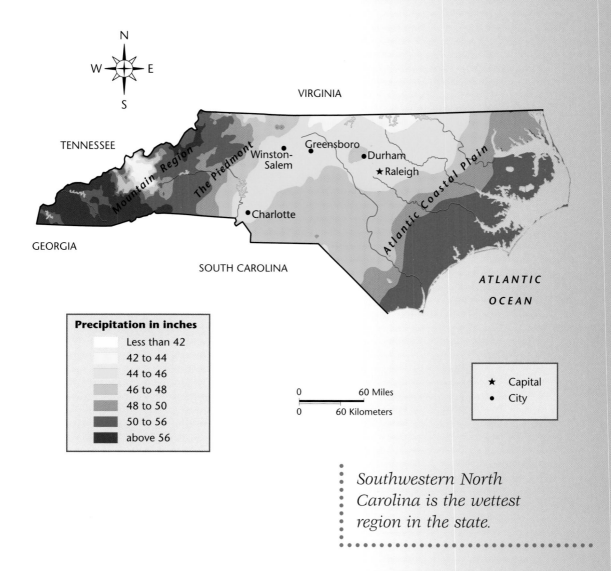

Southwestern North Carolina is the wettest region in the state.

about 40 inches of precipitation a year. The wettest areas, in the mountainous west, get more than 100 inches. Most of North Carolina's precipitation falls in the form of rain, but it can snow anywhere in the state in winter. The northern Piedmont area averages 10 inches of snow a year, while some of the higher mountains average 50 inches.

# Famous Firsts

In 1585 the English started their first North American settlement on Roanoke Island. This first **colony** failed, but a second was started in 1587. Shortly after the second colony's founding, a baby girl was born to one of the settlers. Named Virginia Dare, she was the first English child to be born in North America. No one knows what happened to Virginia. Within a few years, both she and the other settlers had disappeared. To this day, no one has an explanation for the colony's disappearance.

On December 17, 1903, at Kitty Hawk, on the Outer Banks, Orville and Wilbur Wright made the first successful airplane flight. For twelve seconds, Orville flew over the windy sands in a machine that the brothers had spent three years designing. The Wrights made only four short flights before a gust of wind wrecked their plane. But what they did opened the skies to everyone.

*This photograph shows the Wright Brothers' flyer taking off on its first flight.*

In 1795 the University of North Carolina was founded at Chapel Hill. Even though the University of Georgia was the first chartered public school, the University of North Carolina was the first public university in the United States to open its doors to students. For the first few weeks of its existence, the university had only one student, Hinton James. Within a month, though, the university had 2 professors and 41 students.

North Carolina has other college firsts. In 1925 the state became home to what is now called North Carolina Central University, the first **liberal arts** college for African Americans to be funded by a state government. In 1941 the state created Pembroke State College, now UNC–Pembroke, the first public university specifically for Native Americans.

The first **gold rush** in the United States took place in North Carolina. In 1799 a boy named Conrad Reed went fishing with his brother and sister in Cabarrus County in the Piedmont Region. He found a large shiny rock in a creek bed and brought it home. It was the first gold nugget found in the United States.

*The Reed Gold Mine, founded by John Reed, is now a historic site. Visitors can pan for gold at a nearby creek.*

John Reed and his family began searching for more gold and thus launched the North Carolina gold rush. Gold seekers from around the world made their way to North Carolina to seek their fortunes. Mines operated in several counties, and the first ever branch of the **U.S. Mint** opened in Charlotte in 1837. The mint produced millions of dollars worth of gold coins until it was closed in 1913. North Carolina's gold rush ended in 1849, when the massive California gold rush of 1849 began.

Pepsi-Cola was first made in New Bern. The cola's inventor, Caleb Bradham, was a pharmacist at a local drug store. At first, he called the soda Brad's Drink, which he made from carbonated water, sugar, vanilla, rare oils, pepsin, and cola nuts. In 1898 he changed the name to something a little catchier: Pepsi-Cola. The drink got its name from the pepsin and the cola nuts in the recipe. The drink was a hit, and by 1905 the first Pepsi-Cola bottling plants had opened in Charlotte and Durham. Today, Pepsi-Cola is the second most popular cola in the world.

# North Carolina's State Symbols

North Carolina's current state flag dates back to 1885.

*The mountains, the ocean, and a three-masted ship on the state seal reflect North Carolina's unique landscapes and its colonial origins.*

## NORTH CAROLINA STATE FLAG

The basic design of North Carolina's first state flag dates back to the **Civil War** (1861–1865). However, the two dates that appear on the flag come from earlier historic events in the state related to the American **Revolutionary War.** May 20, 1775, the date of the Mecklenburg Declaration of Independence. This is the day the residents of Mecklenburg County declared independence from Great Britain when the state was still a colony. Many people say this event never happened, that it is a myth, yet the date still appears on the flag. On April 12, 1776, the date of the Halifax Resolves, North Carolina agreed that **delegates** to the **Continental Congress** should vote for American independence.

## NORTH CAROLINA STATE SEAL

The current state seal was adopted in 1971. On the left is a woman who represents Liberty, and the seated woman on the right represents Plenty, a symbol of all the abundant riches that can be found in the state. The dates of the Mecklenburg Declaration and the Halifax Resolves also appear on the seal. At the bottom of the seal is the state motto, *Esse quam videri.*

## State Motto: *Esse Quam Videri*

The North Carolina state motto is *Esse quam videri,* a Latin phrase that means "To be rather than to seem." The motto signifies the honesty and integrity of the people of North Carolina. The state government adopted this motto in 1893. Until then, North Carolina was one of the few states without a motto.

## State Nickname: Tar Heel State

North Carolina's nickname is the Tar Heel State. In colonial times, **pine tar** was one of North Carolina's main products. According to one story, North Carolinians began to be known as Tar Heels during the Civil War. After one battle, a group of North Carolina soldiers fought back some Union troops alone. Later they taunted soldiers from Virginia, who were supposed to have helped them. The North Carolina soldiers joked that the Virginians would need to have tar put on their heels so that they would "stick" around during the next battle. A general who heard this story called the North Carolina soldiers Tar Heel Boys, and the name caught on.

## State Flower: Flowering Dogwood

The North Carolina General Assembly named the flowering dogwood the state flower in 1941. This flower grows on the dogwood tree, one of the most prevalent types of trees in the state. The blooms of the dogwood come in shades of white and pink.

*Dogwoods bloom in the spring and into the summer.*

## "The Old North State"

Carolina! Carolina! heaven's blessings attend her,

While we live we will cherish, protect, and defend her,

Tho' the scorner may sneer at and witlings defame her,

Still our hearts swell with gladness whenever we name her.

Hurrah! Hurrah! the Old North State forever,

Hurrah! Hurrah! the good Old North State.

### STATE SONG: "THE OLD NORTH STATE"

Before it became known as the Tar Heel State, North Carolina had a different nickname: The Old North State. This nickname is also the title of the official state song. The song was written by William Gaston, and the music was arranged by Mrs. E. E. Randolph. The song was adopted by the state government in 1927.

### STATE TREE: PINE TREE

The state tree of North Carolina is the pine tree. It is the most common tree in the state. By providing tar, **pitch,** and **turpentine,** the pine tree played an important role in North Carolina's economy during colonial times. These products were important for merchants as well as shipbuilders.

### STATE BIRD: CARDINAL

The cardinal is the official state bird. It lives in the state year round. Male cardinals are known for their bright red feathers and

*The pine tree was named the state tree in 1963.*

black mask around their bills. Female cardinals are not as brightly colored as male cardinals. The duller color helps the female blend into the surroundings so that she can protect her eggs.

*The Plott hound is known for its unusual call, which some people say sounds like a bugle.*

## STATE DOG: PLOTT HOUND

North Carolina adopted the Plott hound as its state dog in 1989. This is the only breed of dog ever developed in the state. Its origins go back to the mid-1700s, when Johannes Plott developed the dog to help him hunt wild boars and bears in the mountains. Today, Plott hounds are still prized as hunting dogs because of their speed.

## STATE MAMMAL: GRAY SQUIRREL

The state mammal, chosen in 1969, is the gray squirrel. The squirrel makes itself at home in almost every part of North Carolina, including its towns and cities.

*Gray squirrels inhabit the woods and parks of the state.*

## STATE REPTILE: EASTERN BOX TURTLE

The eastern box turtle, native to the southern Appalachians, is North Carolina's state reptile. It lives mostly in meadows and wooded areas, but it often prefers moist areas, such as springs and streams. The turtle helps to keep the waters of the state clean by feeding on insects. The eastern box turtle was named the state turtle in 1979.

*Eastern box turtles can live for 60 years or more.*

*North Carolina's mountains provide the state with granite, chosen as the state rock in 1979.*

## STATE INSECT: HONEYBEE

North Carolina's state insect is the honeybee. This bee makes two important contributions to the state's economy. It produces more than $2 million worth of honey per year, and it helps pollinate the crops that North Carolina farmers grow. The honeybee was named the state insect in 1973.

## STATE ROCK: GRANITE

Granite is the official state rock. North Carolina has plenty of it, including the world's largest open-face granite **quarry.** The quarry, near Mount Airy, is a mile long and 1,800 feet wide. Because of its strength, granite is very useful in buildings. North Carolina granite has been used in structures throughout the country, including the gold depository at Fort Knox.

## STATE VEGETABLE: SWEET POTATO

The sweet potato was named the official state vegetable in 1995. North Carolina is the largest producer of sweet potatoes in the country. Farmers harvest more than four billion pounds each year.

*The North Carolina state quarter was the twelfth state quarter to be released—just as North Carolina was the twelfth state admitted to the Union.*

## NORTH CAROLINA STATE QUARTER

North Carolina's state quarter, issued in 2001, shows the Wright Brothers flying their plane for the first time at Kitty Hawk. The quarter shows the year 1789, when North Carolina **ratified** the U.S. Constitution.

# North Carolina's History and People

**P**eople first entered what is now North Carolina 10,000 years ago. These people were descendants of those who came to North America during the **Ice Age.**

## FIRST INHABITANTS

North Carolina's first inhabitants were Native Americans. Thirty tribes lived in the state before European people arrived. Algonquian tribes such as the Roanoc and the Hatteras lived in the northeastern part of the state. Most of the Atlantic coastal plain region was inhabited by the Tuscarora, and the Piedmont was home to several smaller tribes. In the west, the Cherokee were the main tribe.

*The Cherokee, a branch of the Iroquois nation, can trace their history in North Carolina back more than a thousand years.*

## EARLY EXPLORERS

The first Europeans to arrive were part of the expedition of Giovanni de Verrazano, who explored the area for France in 1524. In the following years, several Spanish expeditions passed through the area, but neither country attempted to set up a **colony.** Sir Walter Raleigh, an English **courtier,** financed an expedition in 1584 to explore the coast of North America for possible settlement.

The first English settlement in North America was established on Roanoke Island in 1585. However, the settlers ran out of supplies the next year and had to return to England. In 1587 another colony was founded on Roanoke. These colonists later vanished mysteriously.

In 1663 England's King Charles II created the Carolina Colony, and in 1712 the colony was split into two parts: North and South. In part, this was because the settlers in the north were different from those in the south. Because the southern city of Charleston was a major seaport, people from the south traveled back and forth from the colony

## The Lost Colony of Roanoke

The second colony of Roanoke Island began in July of 1587 with 90 men, 17 women, and 9 children. When the colony required more food and supplies for survival, its governor, John White, went back to England to ask for more supplies. By the time he got back, the colonists had vanished. The only trace found of them was the word *croatoan* scrawled on a tree trunk. Historians have debated what the word *croatoan* reveals about the fate of the lost colony. Some think the colonists were killed by Native Americans, but others believe they began living with the Croatan people.

to Europe. Settlers in the north did not travel as much or come into contact with many Europeans.

## THE REVOLUTIONARY WAR

North Carolinians grew frustrated under the rule of the English king. Like other colonists, they did not like having to pay taxes to the king. They decided to take action toward gaining independence from England, and thus the **Revolutionary War** (1775–1783) began. On April 12, 1776, the North Carolina Provincial Congress passed the Halifax Resolves, which stated that North Carolina's **delegates** to the Continental Congress could declare independence from Great Britain along with the other colonies. North Carolina was the first colony to take this step toward independence through revolution.

North Carolina did its fair share during the Revolutionary War, providing about 6,000 soldiers for the army. North Carolina was the site of one of the most important battles in the war. In 1781 the colonists fought the British at Guilford Courthouse. Even though the British won the battle, they suffered so many losses that they left North Carolina. North Carolina was free.

## STATEHOOD

Although North Carolina had been the first colony to declare independence from England, it was one of the last of the thirteen colonies to **ratify** the U.S. Constitution. North Carolina was slow to ratify in part because the Constitution did not have wording to protect the rights of individual citizens, such as freedom of religion and speech. In November 1789, after Congress proposed a series of **amendments** to the Constitution, North Carolina joined the Union as the twelfth state.

## THE CIVIL WAR

In 1860 about one-third of the people of North Carolina were slaves. However, most North Carolinians did not

*General Joseph E. Johnston surrendered his army of 30,000 troops to Major General William T. Sherman in the home of James Bennett near Raleigh on April 26, 1865.*

own slaves. President Lincoln and many people in the northern states were opposed to slavery. When the **Civil War** broke out in 1861, North Carolina supported the Union. However, when President Lincoln asked the states still in the Union to supply 75,000 **militia,** North Carolina did not because it did not want to fight its southern neighbors. Thus, North Carolina chose to fight on the **Confederate** side, and, on May 20, 1861, **seceded.** After the war ended, North Carolina officially rejoined the United States in July 1868.

## NORTH CAROLINA AND CIVIL RIGHTS

For many years after the Civil War, North Carolina denied its African American citizens their constitutional rights.

*Franklin McCain, Joseph McNeil, Ezell Blair Jr., and David Richmond were all teenagers when they protested segregation in North Carolina.*

African Americans could not attend certain schools and universities, and public areas were **segregated.** The situation for African Americans began to change in the 1950s, but integration did not occur until the late 1960s and early 1970s.

North Carolina has been a part of some important civil rights firsts. On February 1, 1960, a group of African American college students sat down at a lunch counter in a Woolworth's store in Greensboro. Only white people were supposed to sit at the counter, so the store refused to serve the African Americans. The students stayed at the counter until the store closed for the day. In the following weeks, hundreds of other students joined them. Elsewhere, African Americans held their own **sit-ins.** In July of 1960 the Greensboro Woolworth ended its policy of segregation. In the years that followed, other stores did the same.

## FAMOUS PEOPLE

**Dolley Payne Madison** (1768–1849), first lady. Born in Guilford County, Dolley Payne married James Madison in 1794. Madison was elected president of the United States in 1809. During the **War of 1812,** the first lady rescued a portrait of George Washington before the British burned down the White House.

*Dolley Madison was popular in the capital, Washington, D.C., hosting many parties for politicians and diplomats.*

**James K. Polk** (1795–1849), U.S. president. Born in Mecklenburg County, James K. Polk was elected president in 1845. He was responsible for expanding the country's borders to include Oregon, California, and much of the southwest.

**O. Henry (William Sidney Porter)** (1862–1910), writer. A native of Greensboro, Porter wrote many short stories under the **pen name** O. Henry, including the famous "Gift of the Magi." His stories were noted for their surprise endings.

**Thomas Wolfe** (1900–1938), novelist. Born in Asheville, Thomas Wolfe became famous for **autobiographical** novels that were set in his native North Carolina. Among his famous novels are *Look Homeward, Angel* and *You Can't Go Home Again.*

*The Asheville boarding house run by Wolfe's mother was home to the author for ten years. It is now a national historic site.*

**Romare Bearden** (1911–1988), artist. Born in Charlotte, Romare Bearden played semiprofessional baseball before turning to art. He moved to New York City and joined the

Harlem Artists Guild, a group for African American artists at the time. His paintings, watercolors, and collages often reflect his childhood in Mecklenburg County. He is best known for his collages, which blend drawings, oils, and photographs to create an original visual experience. Many of his works now hang in Charlotte's Mint Musuem of Art.

**Billy Graham** (1918–  ), **evangelist.** Billy Graham is one of the most famous preachers in the United States. He has conducted **crusades** all over the world. Born in Charlotte, Graham is a popular speaker, and his television specials, called *The Billy Graham Crusade,* are broadcast all over the world.

**Andy Griffith** (1926–  ), actor. Andy Griffith grew up in Mount Airy, a small town in northwestern North Carolina. After he became a successful actor, he starred in his own TV series, *The Andy Griffith Show.* It became one of the most popular series of all time. Griffith set the show in the fictional town of Mayberry. People have always thought that Mayberry was modeled after Mount Airy. Today, tourists can visit Mount Airy to see "Mayberry" for themselves. Griffith later starred in the television series *Matlock,* about a southern lawyer.

**Elizabeth Hanford Dole** (1936–  ), politician. Born in Salisbury, Dole has held six different positions under six presidents. In 1991 she was named the chairperson of the American Red Cross. Her husband, Senator Bob Dole, ran for president in 1996 but lost. In 2002 North Carolinians elected Elizabeth Dole as their first woman U.S. Senator.

**Michael Jordan** (1963–  ), basketball player. Michael Jordan grew up in Wilmington. He won a basketball scholarship to the University of North Carolina in Chapel Hill (UNC). He then went on to play for the Chicago Bulls. While with the Bulls, his team won six NBA championships, and he is generally considered the greatest basketball player of all time.

*Elizabeth Dole was the first woman to serve as Secretary of Transportation, from 1983 to 1987.*

*Michael Jordan led the U.S. basketball team to Olympic gold medals in 1984, in Los Angeles, and in 1992, in Barcelona, Spain.*

# Biltmore Estate

It might seem surprising to find a palace in the mountains of North Carolina. Yet, just outside of Asheville is a house so spectacular that "palace" is the right word to describe it. The Biltmore estate is the largest private home in the United States.

## The Largest Home in the United States

The story of the Biltmore estate goes back to the late 1800s. George Washington Vanderbilt was the grandson of Cornelius Vanderbilt, who had become rich by building railroads. George Vanderbilt visited North Carolina with his mother in 1888. He fell in love with the land and the climate, so he used his family money to build a large country home there. He bought 125,000 acres of land in the North Carolina mountains and paid an architect to design a house for him.

*The Biltmore House contains art and furniture that date back to the 1400s. It is also a National Historic Landmark.*

Work began on the house in 1889, and by 1895 it was finished. The house had 250 rooms, including 43 bathrooms, 65 fireplaces, and 3 kitchens. Vanderbilt named his new estate Biltmore. The name is a combination of two words. *Bilt* refers to the part of the Netherlands that the Vanderbilt family came from. *More* is an old English word for "rolling hills." A brick factory had to be opened nearby to meet the building demands, and limestone was brought by train from Indiana.

*In the spring, Biltmore's Azalea Garden comes alive with acres of red, pink, and white flowers. It is the largest collection of native azaleas in the United States.*

## THE GARDENS

George Vanderbilt hired Frederick Law Olmsted, the famous landscape architect who designed New York's Central Park, to design the estate's grounds. Part of Olmsted's design included large gardens. Different parts of the gardens have different themes: one area focuses on flowering shrubs called azaleas. The Biltmore gardens include a rose garden, where 200 types of roses bloom. The grounds also feature a wooded, 250-acre deer park where animals can roam.

## A MUSEUM OPEN TO THE PUBLIC

Today, the Biltmore estate remains a private home, but it is open to the public. Every year, around a million visitors come to see the house, admire the gardens, and stroll through the forests. The Biltmore estate also has the most visited winery in the country. Here, award-winning wines are made from the grapes that grow on the estate. Those with some extra money to spend can even stay at a hotel on the estate.

# North Carolina's State Government

**L**ike the U.S. government, North Carolina's government is divided into three branches: legislative, executive, and judicial. Also like the U.S. government, North Carolina has a **constitution.** Among other things, the constitution declares that all people are created equal. The state government is centered in Raleigh, the state capital.

## LEGISLATIVE BRANCH

The legislative branch makes North Carolina's laws. North Carolina's **legislature** is called the General Assembly. Like the U.S. Congress, it is divided into two parts: the senate and the house of representatives. The senate has 50 members, and the house has 120 members. Both senators and representatives are elected to two-year terms in office.

*North Carolina's capitol building dates back to 1833.*

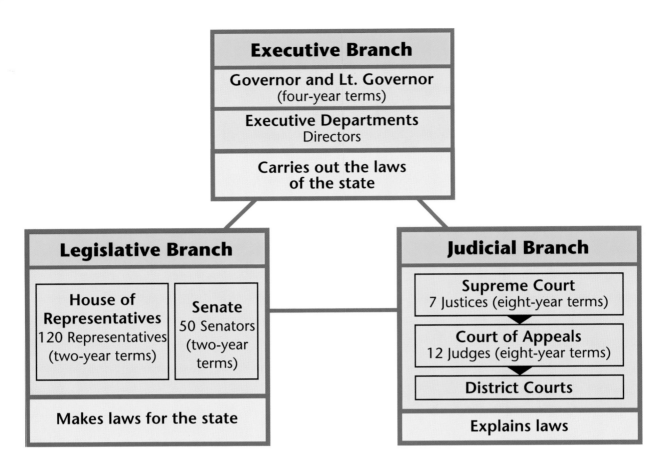

**Executive Branch**

Governor and Lt. Governor
(four-year terms)

Executive Departments
Directors

Carries out the laws
of the state

**Legislative Branch**

House of Representatives
120 Representatives
(two-year terms)

Senate
50 Senators
(two-year terms)

Makes laws for the state

**Judicial Branch**

Supreme Court
7 Justices (eight-year terms)

Court of Appeals
12 Judges (eight-year terms)

District Courts

Explains laws

For a **bill** to become a law in North Carolina, it has to be passed by majorities in both the house and the senate. It then goes to the governor for approval. For many years, North Carolina's governor was the only state governor without the power to **veto** a bill. Since 1997, when the laws were changed, the governor has been able to veto bills passed by the General Assembly. The Assembly can reverse a veto by having three-fifths of the members of each house vote in favor of the bill again.

## EXECUTIVE BRANCH

The executive branch runs the state government and enforces its laws. At the head of the executive branch is the governor, whom the voters of North Carolina elect to a four-year term. The lieutenant governor assists the governor but is elected separately. The executive branch also includes eighteen departments that handle different areas of state government. Some of these offices include the **attorney general,** the **secretary of state,** and the **treasurer.** The heads of these departments are in the governor's **cabinet.** Some of the department heads, such as the attorney general, are elected, while others, such as the head of public safety, are chosen by the governor.

## JUDICIAL BRANCH

North Carolina's judicial branch interprets the laws passed by the General Assembly and applies them in real situations. This branch is broken down into three divisions, from lowest to highest. The lowest courts are the district courts. The district courts are responsible for hearing cases where a minor law has been broken or where someone is being sued for less than $10,000. District court judges are elected and serve four-year terms. The superior courts handle cases where someone is accused of committing a serious crime, such as murder or robbery, or where one party is suing another for more than $10,000. Superior court judges are elected to serve eight-year terms.

The third division of the judicial branch is the Appellate Division. This division hears **appeals** of the decisions handed down in lower court trials. It consists of two courts. The first is the Court of Appeals, which includes fifteen judges. They sit on three-person panels that listen to appeals from the lower courts. The second appellate court is the North Carolina Supreme Court. The supreme court has a total of seven members, including one chief justice and six other justices. The decisions it hands down cannot be appealed any further on the state level, though such cases can be appealed to the U.S. Supreme Court. North Carolina Supreme Court judges are elected for eight-year terms.

*The North Carolina Supreme Court meets in the Justice building in Raleigh.*

# North Carolina's Culture

**N**orth Carolina offers many cultural events throughout the state. These festivals and gatherings reflect the diverse heritages of the people of North Carolina.

### CHEROKEE CULTURE

The Cherokee have called North Carolina home for hundreds of years. Each year, these Native Americans hold the Cherokee Indian Fair in Cherokee, North Carolina. The fair features music, exhibits, and carnival rides. But what truly makes this festival unique is its focus on celebrating Cherokee culture. There are blowgun and archery competitions and Indian stickball games. Vendors sell hot fried bread, a Cherokee treat. The fair even features a Miss Cherokee pageant.

In addition to the fair, throughout the year the Cherokee present an outdoor play called *Unto These Hills.* The play, set in the Smoky Mountains, begins with the story of how the Cherokee first encountered Spanish explorers in 1540. The play portrays how, in the 1800s, the Cherokee were forcefully removed from their homeland in what became known as the **Trail of Tears.** Cherokee descendants play crucial roles in the play, which also features many Cherokee dances.

*The Cherokee play* Unto These Hills *has been seen by more than five million people since it opened in 1950.*

## HIGHLAND GAMES

The Grandfather Mountain Highland Games celebrate the Scottish heritage of many of the state's residents. Such games originated in Scotland in the 1000s. Many Scottish immigrants made their way to North Carolina and brought these traditions with them. The games were officially started in 1956, but many games can be traced back to before the **Revolutionary War.** The games feature traditional dancing and bagpipe playing, sheepdog-herding contests, and athletic events, including the traditional foot race around a 440-yard oval track. Men wear kilts, which are skirts with Scottish **tartan** designs on them. Visitors can also learn Gaelic, the language spoken by the Scottish. The games are held every August.

*The Grandfather Mountain Highland Games inspired similar games in other states, including Florida and Tennessee.*

## OTHER FESTIVALS

The National Hollerin' Contest in Spivey's Corner is a throwback to the days before telephones, when the best way of talking to a neighbor was to shout back and forth across the fields. About 5,000 people gather each year to watch or take part in contests to see who has the best and loudest holler. The special day features a Whistlin' Contest, the Junior Hollerin' Contest for young people, the Ladies Callin' Contest for women, and, of course, the National Hollerin' Contest.

# North Carolina's Food

**N**orth Carolina has a distinctly southern heritage when it comes to food. Specialties such as pork barbeque, southern fried chicken, and sweet potato pie are traditional regional foods.

## Hush puppies

A good side dish for barbecue is hush puppies, little deep-fried balls of cornmeal. According to one story, hush puppies got their name because people would toss these balls to their dogs to fill them up and keep them quiet. Somewhere along the line, someone figured out that hush puppies were worth keeping on the table.

### BARBECUE PORK

North Carolina is famous for its barbecue pork. There are two styles of Carolina barbecue: eastern and western. Both styles use pork but with very different-tasting sauces. Eastern-style barbecue uses a vinegar-based sauce with hot peppers in it. The English made ketchups with vinegar, mushrooms, and sometimes oysters in them. They are probably likely ancestors

*Barbecuing first became popular in Lexington, where people would roast wild pigs over an open fire. Lexington is now considered the barbecue capital of North Carolina.*

# Sweet Potato Pie

**Be sure to have an adult help you with this recipe!**

2 cups cooked, mashed sweet potatoes

1 cup firmly packed brown sugar

1/2 stick butter

2 eggs, beaten

1 cup half-and-half

1 tablespoon lemon juice

1 teaspoon cinnamon

1/2 teaspoon allspice

1 prepared pie crust

Preheat the oven to 400°F. Line a 9- or 10-inch pie plate with pie crust. Combine sweet potatoes and sugar. Melt butter. Combine melted butter and eggs with sweet potatoes. Add half-and-half, lemon juice, cinnamon, and allspice and mix well. Bake at 400°F for 10 minutes and then reduce heat to 350°F and bake for 45 to 50 more minutes.

of the eastern-style barbecue sauce. Western-style barbecue uses a tangy, smoky tomato sauce.

## SWEET POTATOES

Another state food is the sweet potato. North Carolina produces more sweet potatoes than any other state in the country. The sweet potato has a long history in the state, too. Native Americans grew the potatoes before the first European settlers arrived in the area. Sweet potatoes are very nutritious, with lots of vitamins A and C. North Carolinians know how to make the most of this vegetable. There are all kinds of sweet potato recipes, including sweet potato casseroles, sweet potato biscuits, and sweet potato pie, a North Carolina favorite.

# North Carolina's Folklore and Legends

**L**egends and folklore are stories that are not totally true but are often based on bits of truth. Often these stories helped people understand things that could not be easily explained. They also taught lessons to younger generations. All peoples have passed down stories as part of their culture.

## WHY THE POSSUM'S TALE IS BARE

A long time ago, the possum had a beautiful, furry tail. He knew it, too, and spent a lot of time bragging about it. The other animals got tired of his bragging and decided to play a trick on him.

The rabbit was the leader. He told the possum that they were going to have a dance in his honor. The rabbit brought along some crickets to help the possum get his tail ready for the big night. The crickets covered the possum's tail as they worked on it. The rabbit told the possum that the crickets were going to keep his tail from getting messy before the dance. What the crickets were really doing was hiding the fact that they were clipping every hair off the possum's tail!

When the possum got to the dance that night, he made a big entrance. He uncovered his tail without looking and began to dance around, singing about how wonderful his tail was. All the other animals laughed. The possum kept on singing about his tail, and the animals laughed even louder. Finally, the possum looked down at his tail. When he saw how bare and thin it was, he rolled over on his back and grimaced, just as a possum does now if it is surprised. The possum learned a lesson: to be more humble about his tail. This folktale also teaches people to be humble about their strong qualities.

## THE MECKLENBERG DECLARATION

Legend has it that in May 1775, during the early days of the American **Revolutionary War,** the Mecklenberg County Committee of Safety wrote a document called the "Mecklenberg Resolves." It stated that the colonists would take small steps to keep order locally until either the Continental Congress or the British Parliament could bring matters under control.

*A monument to the legend of the Mecklenberg Declaration stands in front of the Mecklenberg County Courthouse.*

More than 40 years later, a few committee members claimed that they had written a declaration of independence from Great Britain. They said that the original document had been lost in a fire. If this were true, the "Mecklenberg Declaration" would have been the first declaration of independence.

# North Carolina's Sports Teams

**A**s recently as the late 1980s, there were no professional sports teams in North Carolina. Since then, things have changed quite a bit. North Carolina is also home to many strong college basketball teams.

### PRO TEAMS

The first major professional team in North Carolina was the Charlotte Hornets of the National Basketball Association (NBA), which started playing in 1988. The Hornets later moved to New Orleans, but the NBA will be returning to the state in 2004. The new Charlotte team, called the Charlotte Bobcats, is already making history. It is the first NBA team to be owned by an African American. Bob Johnson, a billionaire who made his money by founding the Black Entertainment Television network, is the owner of the new team.

Other pro sports have come to North Carolina, too. The Charlotte Sting represent the state in the Women's National Basketball Association (WNBA). The Carolina Panthers of the National Football League (NFL) also play in Charlotte, at Ericsson Stadium. The Carolina Hurricanes of the National Hockey League (NHL) play in

*In 1997 the Carolina Hurricanes moved to North Carolina from Hartford, Connecticut.*

Raleigh. In 2002 the Hurricanes brought the excitement of play-off hockey to North Carolina, making it all the way to the Stanley Cup Finals.

## COLLEGE TEAMS

College sports are popular in the state. North Carolina has its share of college football fans, but North Carolinians go crazy over basketball. Four colleges in the state are traditional basketball powers: the University of North Carolina (UNC) Tar Heels in Chapel Hill, the North Carolina State Wolfpack in Raleigh, the Wake Forest Demon Deacons in Winston-Salem, and the Duke Blue Devils in Durham. All the universities are members of the Atlantic Coast Conference, and except for Wake Forest, they have all won national championships. Since 1979 Duke and UNC have each won three titles, and they have combined for seventeen appearances in the Final Four of the national tournament. The

*Michael Jordan averaged 17.7 points per game while a player at UNC, and led the Tarheels to the National Championship in 1982.*

campuses of Duke and North Carolina are only ten miles apart, and the rivalry between the two teams is intense.

North Carolina's schools also have many excellent women's teams. The UNC women won the NCAA basketball championship in 1993. The biggest college sports dynasty in the state is also at UNC. The school's women's soccer team has won eighteen national championships. At one point, they went 103 games without a loss! In 2003, UNC won the national championship and finished the season with a 27–0 record, the best team record in NCAA women's soccer history.

# North Carolina's Businesses and Products

**N**orth Carolina's economy was once dominated by agricultural products, but in the 1900s North Carolina became a leader in many manufacturing industries, including furniture and **textiles.** Today, technology and financial industries are also central to the state's economy.

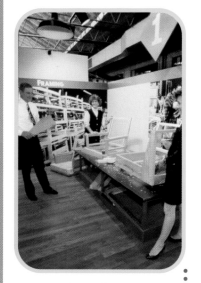

*Located in downtown High Point, the Furniture Discovery Center is the nation's only museum of furniture design and manufacturing.*

## INDUSTRY AND MANUFACTURING

Though the textile industry in North Carolina has fallen on difficult times, North Carolina still leads the nation in furniture production. This industry is centered in High Point, the "furniture capital of America." Furniture making is so important to the economy that High Point has a museum, the Furniture Discovery Center, devoted to the history of furniture making in North Carolina.

Another of North Carolina's largest manufacturing industries is tobacco production. The farms in the state have grown tobacco for hundreds of years. Today, North Carolina factories produce millions of tobacco products each day. The R. J. Reynolds Tobacco Company, in Winston Salem, runs two of the biggest tobacco facilities in the world.

Many other industries and companies are based in North Carolina. The state is a leading center for research and

# Washington Duke

The biggest name in the **industrialization** of North Carolina was Washington Duke. After the **Civil War,** Duke started a small tobacco factory on his farm outside of present-day Durham. By 1880, his business had grown into a national corporation, the American Tobacco Company. In 1884 the factories run by Duke and his sons started using high-tech machines. The increased production made Duke a wealthy man.

Washington Duke and his two sons used the family's money for many good causes. Indeed, they put most of their money into education. Duke gave hundreds of thousands of dollars to help move a small college to Durham. Part of the gift was based on the condition that the school admit women as students. Later gifts helped turn the college into a large university, which was then named for the family. Today, Duke University is one of the best universities in the United States.

technology in the fields of computers, communications, health, and science. Research Triangle Park, between Raleigh and Durham, is home to many leading technology and research firms including Eli Lilly and IBM. The state is a leader in the finance industry and thus is headquarters to many companies that offer banking, real estate, investment, and insurance services. Nationsbank and First Union have their headquarters in the state. Other companies that call North Carolina home are Lowe's, a home-improvement store, and Food Lion, a national grocery store chain.

*North Carolina is still the biggest tobacco-producing state in the nation.*

North Carolina farms raise many animals for food, including hogs and cattle. In 1995 the state led the nation in turkey production. More than 1.5 billion pounds of turkey were sold, worth more than $500 million. Chickens, or broilers, are also important to the economy. North Carolina ranks fourth in broiler production in the United States.

# Research Triangle Park

The Research Triangle Park sits on more than 7,000 acres of land in between the cities of Raleigh, Durham, and Chapel Hill. The park was established in the late 1950s as a way to attract scientific and technological organizations to the state. Howard Odum, professor of sociology at the University of North Carolina at Chapel Hill, proposed several formats that incorporated the idea of cooperation among research organizations. Romeo Guest was also very interested in the idea of creating a research park, and he was one of the first people to use the name Research Triangle Park.

Part of the park's success comes from the fact that it is close to three major universities. Chapel Hill has the University of North Carolina, Durham has Duke University, and Raleigh has North Carolina State University. Together, the universities provide expertise in areas ranging from medicine to **engineering** to environmental sciences.

Among the more than 130 companies that have offices in the research triangle are IBM, Cisco, and Nortel, companies that conduct computer and information technology research. The park is also home to Eli Lilly, which does research on medications, and Reichhold, which does chemical research.

## MILITARY

North Carolina is home to many military bases, including the army base at Fort Bragg in Fayetteville, the marines base at Camp Lejeune in Jacksonville, and Seymour Johnson Air Force Base in Goldsboro. Almost 100,000 military personnel are stationed in the state, and more than 70,000 of those servicemen and servicewomen are stationed at Fort Bragg. Because of the heavy military presence in the state, North Carolina firms receive billions of dollars in defense contracts.

# Attractions and Landmarks

**N**orth Carolina is full of interesting places to visit. Historic sites and other attractions dot the state from the ocean to the mountains.

## COASTAL ATTRACTIONS

Cape Hatteras Lighthouse is on Hatteras Island on the Outer Banks. At 208 feet in height, it is the tallest lighthouse in the nation. Visitors flock to the top to enjoy the view of Hatteras Island and the waters that surround it. The beacon from the lighthouse can be seen for twenty miles out at sea.

*Cape Hatteras Lighthouse is open to the public from April until mid-October.*

The lighthouse is located about three miles from Diamond Shoals, a dangerous area of shallow water

# Moving Cape Hatteras Lighthouse

When Cape Hatteras Light was built, it was 1,500 feet from the waves. By the early 1980s, the ocean was only 70 feet away due to **erosion.** In June 1999, after years of planning, workers began to move the lighthouse more than a half mile to protect it from further erosion. The lighthouse was lifted up onto rails and moved slowly. Its top speed was no more than a few hundred feet a day, and it moved only five feet at a time. By July, the lighthouse was safely in its new location, and it was reopened to the public the following year. Today, it stands a safe 1,600 feet away from the shoreline.

just off Cape Hatteras. Since Europeans first explored the area in the late 1500s, more than 600 ships have sunk in the waters off the Outer Banks. Taking such a toll on shipping earned Cape Hatteras the nickname Graveyard of the Atlantic. Cape Hatteras Lighthouse was opened in 1870 to serve as a reliable guide for ships trying to make their way through the difficult waters.

The Wright Brothers National Monument at Kitty Hawk celebrates the first flight of Orville and Wilbur Wright, on December 17, 1903. Today, a granite boulder marks the spot where the first flight left the ground. Other markers

*A tall granite monument on top of Kill Devil Hill commemorates the Wright brothers' first flight.*

# Places to See in North Carolina

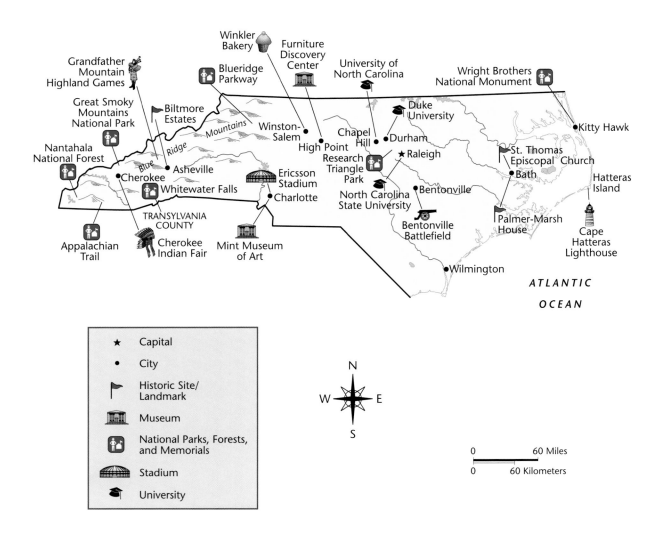

**Legend:**
- ★ Capital
- • City
- ⚑ Historic Site/ Landmark
- 🏛 Museum
- National Parks, Forests, and Memorials
- Stadium
- University

0 ———— 60 Miles
0 ———— 60 Kilometers

show the distance of each of the four flights. The memorial includes Kill Devil Hill, a 90-foot tall sand dune that the Wright Brothers used as their launch site. Also at the site are reconstructions of buildings used by the Wrights during their stays at Kill Devil Hills. One is similar to the building they used as a hangar for their first flyer.

## HISTORIC NORTH CAROLINA

A little farther inland lies Bath, the oldest town in North Carolina. Bath was founded in 1705 and has been lived in ever since. The town is home to many historic buildings, including the Saint Thomas Episcopal Church, which is the oldest surviving church in North Carolina.

## The Nation's Safest Beach

North Carolina's White Lake, located near the town of Elizabethtown, provides unusual swimming conditions. No rivers flow into or out of the lake. Instead, it is fed by underground springs. Because of this water source, the water is clear enough to see to the bottom of the lake even at its deepest parts. The lake bottom is sandy and smooth, with no rocks or holes. Because there are no currents or tides, there is nothing to pull against swimmers and waders. For this reason, the lake has been called the "nation's safest beach."

Another of Bath's historic buildings is the Palmer-Marsh House. Built in the mid-1700s, it is one of the oldest buildings in the state. One of the unusual features of the house is its double chimney, which takes up much of one side of the house. Two chimneys allowed the house to stay warm during the winter months. The chimney is four feet thick and up to seventeen feet wide. There are even two small windows set in the chimney to allow light into the rooms inside.

Winston-Salem is a modern city with a historic core. In the downtown area of the city are more than 90 historic buildings built in the 1700s and 1800s. They were part of the town of Salem, founded in 1766 by German-speaking immigrants known as Moravians. Today, visitors can tour historic homes and businesses to see what life was like for early settlers in the Piedmont. One of the most popular tourist stops is the Winkler Bakery, where visitors can buy fresh bread and cookies baked Moravian style. Moravian-style cookies are very thin and baked with spices such as cloves, cinnamon, ginger, and nutmeg.

*Built in 1800 by Johann Gottlob Krause, the Winkler Bakery has been in operation for more than 100 years.*

*Whitewater Falls are inside Nantahala National Forest.*

## WESTERN NORTH CAROLINA

In the western part of the state, near the South Carolina border, visitors can see Transylvania County's Whitewater Falls, the highest waterfall east of the Rocky Mountains. Whitewater Falls is actually two separate waterfalls. The upper set of falls drops 411 feet over a rocky wall. The lower half of the falls, which is actually in South Carolina, drops another 200 feet. Whitewater Falls is not the only waterfall in Transylvania County. Because more than 200 waterfalls lie within the county's borders, its nickname is Land of Waterfalls.

Great Smoky Mountains National Park is the most visited national park in the country. The park covers more than 500,000 acres, and extends into Tennessee. The Appalachian Trail, a trail that runs from Maine to Georgia, weaves its way through the Great Smoky Mountains National Park. The trail runs for 200 miles in North Carolina.

## Blueridge Parkway

Many visitors see the sights of North Carolina from the Blueridge Parkway, a road that showcases much of the wonderful mountain scenery in the state. The road was started in 1935 and provided jobs for many people during the **Great Depression.** The 200-mile road runs through the state and connects the Great Smoky National park with the Shenandoah National Park in Virginia.

# Map of North Carolina

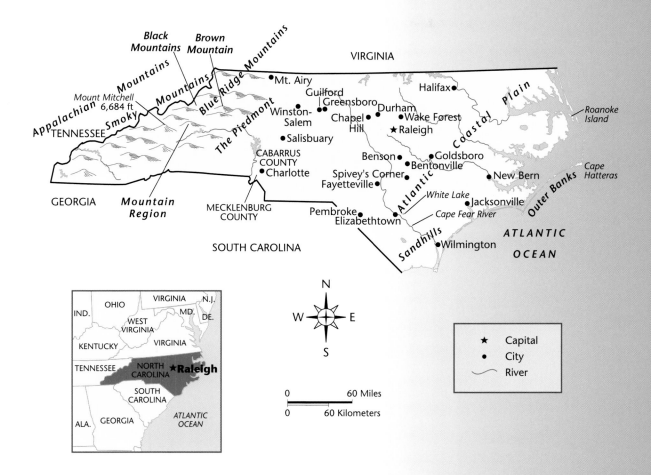

Black Mountains

Brown Mountain

Blue Ridge Mountains

Appalachian Mountains

Mountains

Mount Mitchell 6,684 ft

VIRGINIA

Smoky

TENNESSEE

The Piedmont

Mt. Airy

Guilford

Winston-Salem

Chapel Hill

Greensboro

Durham

Wake Forest

★ Raleigh

Halifax

Coastal Plain

Roanoke Island

Salisbuary

CABARRUS COUNTY

Charlotte

Benson

Bentonville

Goldsboro

New Bern

Cape Hatteras

GEORGIA

Mountain Region

MECKLENBURG COUNTY

Spivey's Corner

Fayetteville

Atlantic

White Lake

Jacksonville

Outer Banks

Pembroke

Elizabethtown

Cape Fear River

SOUTH CAROLINA

Sandhills

Wilmington

ATLANTIC OCEAN

OHIO

VIRGINIA

N.J.

IND.

MD.

DE.

WEST VIRGINIA

KENTUCKY

VIRGINIA

TENNESSEE

NORTH CAROLINA

★Raleigh

SOUTH CAROLINA

ALA.

GEORGIA

ATLANTIC OCEAN

N
W        E
S

0        60 Miles

0        60 Kilometers

★   Capital
•   City
⁀   River

# Glossary

**amendments** additions or changes to a document

**appeals** cases brought before a higher court for a review of the decision of a lower court

**attorney general** chief law officer of a state or nation

**autobiographical** the story or someone's life, written by that person

**barrier islands** small islands that are near the mainland and protect it from the full force of the ocean

**bill** proposed law to be considered for approval by lawmakers

**cabinet** a group of people chosen by a leader to help him or her run a government

**capes** areas of land that extend into a body of water

**Civil War** the war between the northern states, called the Union, and the southern states, known as the Confederacy, fought between 1861 and 1865

**colony** a region controlled by a far-away country

**Confederate** a person who supported the Confederacy, or southern states, during the Civil War

**constitution** a plan of government for a state or nation that describes how a government works, makes laws, and grants freedoms

**Continental Congress** from 1774-1789 the federal legislature of the thirteen colonies and later of the United States

**courtier** a person who attends a royal court

**crusades** movements for a cause

**delegates** elected or chosen representatives

**engineering** the science of designing and making complex products

**erosion** gradual wearing away of rock or soil caused by water, wind, or ice

**evangelist** a person who spreads the Christian gospel

**gold rush** a large movement of people to an area where gold has been discovered

**Great Depression** period of American history in the 1930s when thee were very few jobs and people struggled for money and food

**humid** full of moisture

**Ice Age** a cold period of time when glaciers covered much of the surface of the earth; the last one ended about 11,000 years ago.

**industrialization** the process of developing the production and sale of goods in an area

**legislature** a group of people responsible for making laws

**liberal arts** college courses that give students general knowledge rather than actual job skills

**militia** people who are trained to be soldiers but who are not part of a regular army

**pen name** a made-up name used by an author

**pine tar** a dark, sticky, oily substance

**pitch** a thick sticky substance that comes from pine sap

**quarry**   an open pit used for obtaining building stone, slate, or marble

**ratify**   to approve something

**Revolutionary War**   the war that the thirteen American colonies fought with Great Britain between 1775 and 1783 to gain their independence

**secede**   declaring that you are no longer part of a country or organization

**secretary of state**   the public official responsible for keeping state records and the state seal

**segregated**   the practice of separated on the basis of some quality, such as race

**temperate**   having a climate that is neither very hot nor very cold

**sit ins**   protests against something in which people sit in a certain place and refuse to move until their requests have been met

**temperate**   having a climate that is neither very hot nor very cold

**textile**   a cloth made by weaving or knitting

**topography**   the surface features of a place

**Trail of Tears**   the route taken by the Cherokee when they were forced to leave their homeland in the 1800s

**treasurer**   the public official in charge of the money of a government

**turpentine**   an oil that comes from the sap and wood of pine trees

**U.S. Mint**   the government agency whose responsibilities include printing coins for the United States

**veto**   the right of a chief executive, such as a governor or president, to reject a law passed by lawmakers

**War of 1812**   a war fought between 1812 and 1814 when Great Britain tried to prevent the United States from trading with France

# More Books to Read

• • • • • • • • • • • • • • • • • • • • • • • • • • • • • • • • • • • • • • • • • • • •

Freedman, Russell. *The Wright Brothers: How They Invented the Airplane.* New York: Holiday House, 1991.

Haley, Gail E. *Mountain Jack Tales.* Boone, N.C.: Parkway Publishers, 2001.

Kummer, Patricia K. *North Carolina (One Nation series).* Mankato, Minn.: Capstone Press, 1998.

Nichols, John. *Cameron Crazies: The Duke Blue Devils Story (College Basketball Today series).* Mankato, Minn.: Creative Education, 1999.

Shirley, David. *North Carlina.* New York: Marshall Cavendish, 2001.

# Index

# About the Authors

Adam McClellan grew up in North Carolina. As a fan of Duke University sports, he has great fun during basketball season but not so much fun when football rolls around. Adam lives in Chapel Hill with his wife and daughter.

Martin Wilson was born and grew up in Alabama. He was educated in Tennessee, Florida, and Texas. Many of his best friends are North Carolinians. He is a writer and editor living in New York City.